THE ROLE OF CHATGPT IN MARKETING MASTERY

THE ROLE OF CHATGPT IN MARKETING MASTERY

BILL VINCENT

RWG Publishing

CONTENTS

1	Introduction to ChatGPT and Marketing	1
2	Foundations of Marketing Mastery	5
3	Applications of ChatGPT in Marketing	9
4	Advanced Techniques and Strategies	13
5	Ethical Considerations in ChatGPT Marketing	17
6	Future Trends and Innovations	20

Copyright © 2024 by Bill Vincent

All rights reserved. No part of this book may be reproduced in any manner whatsoever without written permission except in the case of brief quotations embodied in critical articles and reviews.

First Printing, 2024

CHAPTER 1

Introduction to ChatGPT and Marketing

The modern society is customer-centric. Enterprises want to reach a lot of customers, obtain detailed marketing information about them, and try to make the products fit the customers' personalized requirements as much as possible to promote the development of the economic society. ChatGPT, as a strong artificial intelligent assistant, not only weakens the estrangement between humans and machines through its text dialog function, but also weakens the estrangement between information and users. With ChatGPT, users can simply communicate with text to inquire about information, make appointments, get services, acquire knowledge, etc., rather than spending minutes searching through web pages to indirectly obtain desired information. The ChatGPT technology revolutionizes the progress of the internet. Through ChatGPT, enterprises can not only provide a variety of environmentally friendly services for users, but also record users' behavior and communication language style, as well as other marketing information, to improve the precision of marketing, make products more personalized, and provide personalized recommendation services.

With the spread of intelligent mobile devices, mobile social software is becoming more and more popular, especially in recent years. The research and development of ChatGPT has been invested a lot of resources by big companies. A new business model, named ChatGPT Commerce, is derived from the ChatGPT technology. A lot of small businesses and individual entrepreneurs rush to leverage the benefits of cooperating with the ChatGPT platform, aiming to achieve high profits with a low budget.

1.1. Understanding ChatGPT Technology

GPT-3 is a very large model, weighing in with 175 billion parameters. But what does that mean? Let's break it down. First, to understand GPT-3, you have to understand that it's a language model. Language models are models that can detect the underlying structure of a language and provide information on how words within the language relate and come together. They are built using deep learning, which is essentially the programming of architecture to mimic the human mind's inner workings, processing lightning-quick calculations in a chip-like fashion. When we say "deep" in "deep learning", that refers to the fact that there are many layers in the neural network where processing occurs. The number of parameters refers to the number of mathematical equations that are configured in the model for deep learning to process. So a model like GPT-3, which has 175 billion parameters, has 175 billion such equations. These equations can handle the interactions among words at such large-scale resolution that they simulate a person's naturally predicated utterances with intense accuracy.

The latest big breakthrough in artificial intelligence (AI) programming is something called GPT-3 (Generative Pre-training Transformer 3). GPT-3 is the third version of OpenAI's GPT series, which uses deep learning to generate human-like text. The original purpose of GPT-3 was to help humans write more effectively by suggesting ways to improve phrasing, academia, and sentence structure. But what is GPT-3 and how exactly does it work?

1.2. Importance of ChatGPT in Marketing

The author Mialki explains that while these models have been proven useful, their effectiveness must be established to the broader group of derived users—to students, teachers, and researchers. Recently, the GPT models have shown promise in marketing and marketing education. Marketing is based on persuasive beliefs, which can serve as initial seeds and serve as gold standards. A person receiving fresh directions and tasks from yourself is one of the consequences that apply the ChatGPT technology known, respectively, as data literacy and artificial intelligence. Marketing expertise remains a high-demand career skill, which requires an understanding of a customer's responses to sales, advertising, and marketing efforts, which are influenced by a variety of psychological and sociological factors. GPT is a pattern defined by a language model, trained to process a language response set, of varying scales and scales, through maturation of size and training data amounts. Clearly, the exponential increase in the amount, scale, scope, and speed of GPTs will pose challenges to regulatory infrastructures.

As an expert in a new AI technology called Generative Pretrained Transformer (GPT), I was glad to read an article by Stephanie Mialki that clarified ChatGPT's definition and explained its origin. GPT-3, only available via limited private beta, is a Generative Pretrained Transformer that is best known for—albeit not limited to—its interactive abilities in which users may communicate much like a human. ChatGPT, such as GPT-3, can be found in a chatbot, in a text message, in exhausted relief, or in fanatic protestation. Unlike GPT-3, ChatGPTs tend to simulate a human conversational style, which is parallel to more trivial and flexible instances and can be trained in order to generate more factual, formal, coarse-grained or fine-grained responses. It is understood as a statistical or mathematical model for generating natural language, trained on a massive dataset of (language, response) pairings.

CHAPTER 2

Foundations of Marketing Mastery

The role of marketing, as a business sub-function, is to facilitate sales through activities such as analysis, planning, implementation of advertising, promotion creation, customer service, customer relationship management, and competitive strategy. Customer outreach through marketing is one of the core competencies to be developed in any business. Digitalization, interactivity, and automation in marketing techniques have strengthened the role of global marketing in modern business management. With the emergence of Artificial Intelligence (AI) and Machine Learning, the use of ChatGPT, a subdivision of OpenAI's GPT (Generative Pre-trained Transformer) models, is increasingly playing a crucial role in B2B marketing. Currently, the cutting edge on GPT models is with Transformer, having the ability to make abstract vector spaces with similar high produced PSLM (prestatistical language model) features across a global scale using unsupervised pretraining fashion.

Marketing, as a concept, is not new. Archaeological evidence suggests that the Romans used murals and advertisements in the form of wooden signs for trade shops. Through the ages, marketing techniques have evolved with the development of commerce and have been closely associated with its evolution. Over time, marketing activities have evolved into many areas such as literacy, competition, efficiency, creativity, social systems, and ethics. With so many aspects involved in this specialist area of business administration, Marketing Mastery can be attributed to nearly everything that a person involved in B2B marketing management is invested in. In the 21st century, there has been increased competition in the marketing segment which led to Marketing Mastery emerging as a thought leader in that space.

2.1. Core Concepts in Marketing

By using a market-oriented perspective, it is possible to identify marketing-relevant interpretations, responsive actions or customer-specific activities—as well as the market opportunities realized. Marketing-oriented firms must combine an understanding of the variability of customer demands with the right organizational responses to appropriate marketing skills. In contemporary marketing, chatbots are regarded as promising digital tools and versatile technologies that offer various marketing benefits to marketing individuals, groups, and organizations. However, chatbot marketing applications also implicate service elements such as personalization and customization through chatbots, and this in turn may influence acceptance, adoption, and usage from the perspective of marketing effectiveness. Nonetheless, little is known about the actual and effective use of chatbots for the purposes of marketing. In other words, the existing research gap is the lack of a clear understanding of the role of chatbots, such as ChatGPT, in the effective utilization of personalization elements in a marketing context.

A marketing orientation has been defined and recommended by marketing academicians and professionals in terms of (1) real customer needs, (2) customer satisfaction, (3) anticipated financial returns for the organization, and (4) an integrated effort throughout the organization. This kind of marketing orientation can lead to superior marketing company performance, identified through the satisfaction of customers and the implementation and execution of marketing activities demanded by customers. Once demands have been identified, sufficient resources, as well as the importance of strong commitment and customer orientation, are devoted to the area of marketing and overall market satisfaction. Marketing is faced with the challenge of fundamentally changing its orientation—or does so at an uncertain cost?

2.2. Digital Marketing Strategies

There are various forms of communication through social media such as ChatGPT, voice call, video call, video conference, and instant message. At present, instant messaging is recognized as a digital or electronic media that is effective and capable of helping public relations in optimizing the communication strategy with external and internal parties of the company. Instant messaging is effective in helping public relations with these advantages. Instant messaging is used to support public relations in conducting various activities such as events, including presentations, digital interactions, media and social monitoring, and Brandwatch. The purpose of these activities is to review the brand's performance and monitor social for thought leadership. Duplication of the results of content makes it easy for public relations to track the metrics of messages that are effectively disseminated.

Electronic media are mediums of direct mass communication with the use of personal computers, laptops, and mobile phones. Digital media or electronic media is very wide, emphasizing the use of personal computers, laptops, and mobile phones. Digital or electronic media can be divided into three, namely media such as print media, broadcast media, and online media. Each of these media has its own characteristics and constraints. If observed carefully, digital media, in comparison to other media used in public relations activities, have more of an impact. Digital media is capable of reaching millions of people, and this has become a more convenient way of communicating. To that end, many public relations activities use digital media in the form of social media. The use of digital media is also used to promote and position products, companies, and organizations. The role and function of social media in public relations effectively facilitate the communications between a company and its stakeholders.

CHAPTER 3

Applications of ChatGPT in Marketing

Automatic marketing savvy assistant Provide a personal marketing-savvy assistant to help direct people toward their content - helping them find the most relevant content or program for their problem. The assistant could learn which topics are addressed in your program and guide prospects to the right program or goal. Not only will it help you become a more integrated part of your client's decision-making process from square one, but it will also show and teach how AI could be used to offer expert-like help in interacting with clients. You give away some knowledge to prospects, create a better user experience, and save time doing support. Any teaching assistant, mentor, or any program director can get a ChatGPT running to ease their countless hours of work in helping someone to decide if a program would make sense for them or where to find the answer within the program. Battle through stereotypes and serve as a proof of concept of how AI can be used to create an incredible, first-level interactive, helping tool for clients.

Research potential newcomers Before joining the program, some learners may have questions that need to be answered. A Chatbot can be mentioned on the main page of Marketing Mastery to welcome newcomers and provide answers to advance questions about the course. If you have case studies about your success and you are selling a product for your clients, you could use ChatGPT to respond to prospective clients on your website to do initial triage of incoming requests and potentially highlight case study results during the interaction.

Use cases of ChatGPT in marketing There are dozens of ways that a tool like Chatbot could be used in marketing, but here's a small subset of possible applications of ChatGPT relevant for a specialized marketing course.

3.1. Content Creation and Personalization

Consumers who are sent an individual advertisement related to an interesting subject do not feel that they are obliged to do something to get their attention, but rather that they receive information about an issue that they are already interested in. However, many systems that collect a marketer with their customers' site provide a generic response that is far from what is needed. To make personalized recommendations for a customer, such methods should reveal their present needs and examine past interactions. However, this can vary the pleasure of a customer's site reached at a particular moment in time. Our work focuses on the use of recommendation models by personalizing it. Instead of waiting for a customer to visit a site before they can get more information about themselves, our method continuously interacts with the customer to update their recommendation personal decision model. In this way, product newsletters on sites/websites and mail can all refer to a personal journey with the efforts made. In particular, users can introduce the abilities of users who are radical and become a credible community.

In what follows, we again visit our previous goals and summarize the method we used. Finally, departmental contributions and research opportunities are discussed.

In today's world that we are living in, the maximum amount of time a potential customer spends on a site is directly proportional to the quality of the personalized content they find on that site. If the customer is not immediately interested in the subject on the page visited, they go to another environment where this expectation is met. For this reason, the subject must be the main point of the title of the article. The advertisement must be shared by individual users according to their interests. Therefore, efforts should be made to establish good social relationships and increase credibility. The naturalness of the content is the main factor that ensures the quality and attractiveness of the promotional material.

3.2. Customer Service and Support

In addition to chatbots, existing zero-shot and zero-training contact with the chatbot model have produced interesting results applied to customer support and the call center. Various companies already use multilingual, large-scale models in customer care, with balanced distribution, and chatbots based on them are demonstrating their effectiveness. Leveraging the models against a system of customer service, we are able to serve different clients speaking different languages, providing customized, responsive support in almost any language across multiple channels. Bring conversational skills to the data and query target guide to next skill tasks.

When it comes to online customer support, automated chatbots are highly efficient and resourceful. The rudimentary way of entering the customer's keyword and trying to extract the best possible information derived from databases, or direct the customer to a human case worker, could serve to provide practical information. The development of a chatbot that uses the language model for customer support will not only lead the customer to a human case worker for more complex questions but also to the current one in topics besides what words-based chatbots can handle. The tool will understand synonyms and have the ability to handle dialogue and retrieve customer queries with better understanding of their immediate needs.

CHAPTER 4

Advanced Techniques and Strategies

In this section, we share some of the marketing techniques that we at Forge Marketing have implemented in our clients and had found successful. First off is the realization that one size does not fit all - successful ChatGPT marketing strategies are achieved through brand individualism. A ChatGPT bot may not possess the breadth of features that a website does. But do not let the magnitude of ChatGPT footnote here fool you. In the sheer brevity of his interaction with your prospects, your ChatGPT bot can leave a lasting impression. What is ChatGPT, and what isn't? You should spare no expense in making sure your ChatGPT users know the answer to this question. For ChatGPT marketing to be successful, a fundamental requirement is that your GPT bot should highlight traits that can generally be ascribed to ChatGPT bots, often, and unreasonably giving away some basic chat skills. In the years ahead, you are going to be competing with hundreds and, eventually, thousands of other responses while looking to ensure, at all costs, that your ChatGPT bots, and your branding, stand out uniquely.

The vanishing barrier to entry has its prices too. The sheer simplicity of ChatGPT's implementation has engendered a mass expansion of ChatGPT-based marketing systems. Successfully navigating this explosive landscape while retaining your brand's essence is not for the lighthearted. Forge Marketing does not profess any profound insight in this endeavor, suffice to say, here is the task before you: in a virtual battlefield clogged with hundreds, possibly thousands, of similar solutions, you must, without the benefit of direct human interaction, make your ChatGPT bots so humane, so approachable, charming, and intelligent that in a market dominated by battlefield competence your brand stands out so head and shoulders above the opposition; you give consumers zero choice but to gravitate towards your branding. We do not champion these difficulties to be discouraging - but as a reminder that the path to ChatGPT marketing mastery is long and narrow and that triumph in this scarcely untamed landscape calls not merely for the leveraging of the readily ChatGPT technological marvel but the appropriation of a vast array of advanced marketing techniques and strategies as well.

4.1. ChatGPT for Market Research

For instance, currently, I can easily figure out the average number of minutes spent in a local bakery or a salon or a small play area apart from the larger retail chains or the movie theaters. This is information that they currently do not have access to. Also, creating surveys is hard to discern why people do what they do. For instance, it has become clear that many fast-food chains encourage dine-ins to increase alcohol consumption but without overbearing, no one is probably going to get candid enough to tell me that clearly in a survey, whereas in a casual conversation mode, I can easily pivot the conversation to alcohol and not even hint that it is stranger. This is a totally skewed result due to question phrasing but leveraging unnamed sources in qualitative conversations can give an empirical insight.

Marketing is an extremely data-driven industry. The role of data has been constantly increasing over the last many years. Now, we have come to a point where without data, it is practically impossible to make any successful marketing dealings. From Google Analytics to various Business Intelligence Tools, agencies have been using different combinations of technology and human intelligence to make the most out of this data. However, certain types of data are not readily available or are relatively more difficult to gather. It is a well-acknowledged fact that qualitative data (especially audio and video) can have much more depth and be more truthful. Think about voice-based assistants or AI. In this context, ChatGPT can be a powerful resource as an AI assistant. Gathering qualitative data, especially at a smaller scale, becomes much simpler. It is easy to build qualitative research questions by brainstorming with peers and then deploying a chatbot to gather data.

4.2. ChatGPT for Predictive Analytics

The directional challenges posed by prediction prevent most CRM projects from failing to meet management objectives, and let's face it, most CRM projects don't. ChatGPT is designed to predict with all the power of the best predictive analytics packages, but its unique added value is its ability to tell you why. In the process of diagnosing what customers will buy and why, you can directly create content where customers will find out or actively encourage them to get that information from you. If salespeople have the knowledge of why customers will make a purchase and have answers to objections already rehearsed, imagined or not, the probability of achieving vision will increase.

Predictive analytics is what differentiates most modern marketing from old school "spray and pray" advertising. There are numerous predictive analytics models out there, variously designed to estimate consumer conversion probability, customer lifetime value, and even customer loyalty. But none of them beat a really good CRM and customer-centric mindset. And even the "best" CRM solutions can be operated by a pretty unimaginative user or absorbed in an end-to-end process that looks like this...

CHAPTER 5

Ethical Considerations in ChatGPT Marketing

We need to embrace our new robotic colleagues with both care and forethought to make sure that they help our employees and customers to have valuable and ethical interactions within the brand conversations. Otherwise, our enthusiastic implementation of robots could actually help to destroy the very organizations that we help to manage today. We need to think about how to prevent potential worker stratification through the use of ChatGPT. For example, implementing company policies to make sure that when a ChatGPT produces something that would raise red flags if published directly, the output should instead trigger an internal alert. When you publish material that will be widely read by the audience, it could contain a subtle sentence that clearly indicates that the source is from a ChatGPT, not a direct-to-brand human origin post. Such alerts could also be checked through a library system that compares the position against a list of known ChatGPT sources, giving your content producers a real-time warning if they are making a mistake. These alerts should also apply to protect internal systems.

Whether we like it or not, robots are here to stay when it comes to retail marketing. They don't need to sleep, they don't need to eat, they don't get sick, and they don't have hangovers. When you can get so much value out of a chat-based AI which is virtually available permanently, it will be very hard for marketing teams to resist going down the path towards implementing chatbots. However, it is important to mitigate against the risks of using these advanced technologies. Putting these bots into your customer service function will alter your team's work roles and could create dissatisfaction or retrenchments among your staff. The use of self-learning AIs raises corporate social responsibility concerns about biases being created in the logic and also the possible misuse of these bots in the future. ChatGPT bots can be used to generate fake news and even to harm others by altering their records without consent, such as doctor's notes on their database.

5.1. Privacy and Data Protection

In online businesses, one of the most important roles is the protection of privacy. It particularly pays more attention to transactions. In Chatbot, conversational dialogues are useful in retrieving specific, transaction-related facts that can be used as input to the database. It answers access and provides support for other remote services. Recognizing customers, the business should aim to use Chatbot to find out customer information like account information, payment status, and physical location. All updates must be recorded in a way that prevents the possibility of unauthorized changes.

In dealing with data processing, it must consider both the free operation of exchange of information and the access to personal data. It also provides proper protection to data-related parties. People, either users or unknowing parties, usually share their data or links with each other. Referring to the chatbot, there are many cases that show the danger that there was a data breach or personal data was shared with bad people. Moreover, using data in an unauthorized manner against the user's expectations and agreement is also considered as data abuse. The existence of personal data can be explored in the conversation of the chatbot.

5.2. Bias and Fairness

What kind of safety and fairness considerations should surround a product created using a huge language model like GPT-3? Safety means that the product is used with minimal unintentional negative effects. If users face unexpected difficulty, the service can get overloaded. Fairness means that every user who the product is designed for can use it successfully. It's useful to organize these considerations as each element in a triage system for the negative effects that the product might cause. Foreseeing potential issues allows for planned, calm fixes, instead of negative surprises forcing rushed stacks of ad hoc solutions. Then, write a product that will not interact with other systems to cause harm, and audits so that users can confirm this.

The most important thing that you should consider when using any artificial intelligence model of large size in practice is the effect that it has. Consider what would happen if a user (unintentionally or intentionally) sent your AI hate speech, false claims, etc. Remember, anything a user puts in, no matter how false and offensive, will be out. Anything your AI says will be publicly associated with you. Although the prompts are vetted, your sales team and web visitors will constantly ask, "What exactly have you trained this on?" Since the prompts are the main source of user interface information, create your documentation by mixing and matching prompt content. First, test GPT-3 in a defined environment, and only use it at a large scale when you understand exactly what it does, which is more sophisticated than it looks.

CHAPTER 6

Future Trends and Innovations

We are looking into more ways that GPT technology can automate content strategy processes, such as automated editorial keyword tagging, temporal filter for freshness of news content, automated ingestion and summarization of financial statements, gisting/summarization of long content with RTF verification, and more. More long-term features we are considering include answer ranking, cascaded intention detection, hybrid KB and passage retrieval for more comprehensive answer coverage, faster and smaller GPT, mixed-language model for mixed-language lines of inquiry. NLP will continue to be a key technology lever for powering data-driven decision-making, support asking complex, multi-line questions and receive responses back that are specific and high-quality from the ChatGPT language model. We thank you for your patience and your continued support of GPT technology.

We are always looking at ways to make our tools more powerful while at the same time making them easier and more efficient to use. We are constantly pushing the boundaries of innovation in search, and our strategies are evolving. But at the same time, we are not able to predict every upgrade that will come down in the future and we certainly can't imagine all the features you will request down the road. Our search functionality serves as a base for providing to our customers the information they are requesting. Given enough time and resources, we should be able to implement improvements and make the product better.

6.1. AI Integration in Marketing

It helps in a much better analysis of credit data and verification of the transaction. AI can provide valuable information about the costs, financial statements, taxes, budgets, and related audit activity. Furthermore, AI can also play a key role in strategic management. It helps in performing market forecasting in a very effective manner. It also helps in creating new business relations, management of a company, organizing response activity, and in strategic and developmental projects. It can suggest new marketing concepts and can help in making the communication process more effective. Using AI, different social and professional segments in the target audience can be identified. It can also help in segmentation, setting up prices for a variety of people, maintaining the brand image, and transferring cognitive knowledge to individuals or groups. In conclusion, AI can be very useful in centralizing the company that wants to cooperate in a new electronic market.

White et al. examined the role of AI in the different components of the marketing strategy. First, they found that AI can identify the potential customers and current competition prevailing in the market. This can be really useful as it would give the company an opportunity to become a monopolist in the industry. AI can help in determining the market trends along with the price changes and searching for new market opportunities. It is also able to provide relevant information regarding the price. In addition, it can link customers, suppliers, technical performance, and brand image. This linking helps in improving the purchasing function and also helps in handling material seamlessly. Moreover, AI can be useful in production planning, scheduling, process monitoring, controlling the quality, service delivery, and providing an after-sales service function. It is also useful in financial management and the decision-making process.

6.2. ChatGPT 4.0 and Beyond

Previous iterations of ChatGPT (1 through 3) improved four major aspects simultaneously: (i) model scale and topology, (ii) multi-modal capabilities, (iii) enablement with the latest optimization methods, and (iv) adjustment with better training datasets covering the evolving types of human conversation. Further iterations can be expected to continue in the same direction. 1. Model scale continues to grow, either to push the state-of-the-art further, to counteract the diminishing returns of added network parameters, both from optimization issues and data quality, or both. 2. Multi-modal capabilities are conveniently "glued" to the generative backbone, allowing the models to benefit from the diverse pre-training stimuli available in the "real" or "distant" supervision. 3. Previous models grew by implementing novel transformer designs first available as research or optimizations were published. It is expected that GPT will continue to implement the state-of-the-art optimization techniques. 4. Finally, yet importantly, data coverage is also paramount in conversation models.

So far, we've mostly discussed working with ChatGPT-3. However, it's not a surprise that many are interested in the details of newer versions such as ChatGPT-4 and beyond. As is so often the case, GPT-4 (and later) will likely become available at some point in the future. Those who have watched (perhaps with envy) as others played with newer, smarter GPT versions have wondered about its capabilities. What changes were introduced in ChatGPT-4? When they can play with the new version, what can they expect? While this is not the place to predict any specifics, we can anticipate some general improvements based on recent research advancements. Note that while "GPT" stands for "Generator Pre-Trained," the simple belief of "GPT" as an optimal system for text completion is often unfounded. (However, "the best" system available is still a pretty good description.)

Milton Keynes UK
Ingram Content Group UK Ltd.
UKHW040938081224
452111UK00011B/225